Leverage To Win

Win

Key Relationships All Men Need To Succeed

the only brother & ... to Kevin & Lane

By Dalton T Beckles
New Hope Clinical Services LLC
2017

Thank you for always being there ... Leverage to Win ...

Ordering Information:
Special discounts are available on quantity purchases by corporations,
associations, and others.
Orders by U.S. trade bookstores and wholesalers. Please visit
daltontbeckles.com. Or email Dalton@newhopeclinical.com

Booking Information
To book Dalton Beckles for your next speaking engagement, please
contact:
Dalton@newhopeclinical.com

1. Spirituality 2. Self-Help
First Edition
Printed in the United States of America

ISBN-13: 978-1977788252

Table of Contents

<u>Note Taking</u>

Book Notes
My Journey to Success

This book is solely based on my own experience. My experience as a social worker, therapist, life coach, husband, father, and son. Throughout my life, I have had personal relationships that have prepared and repaired me to succeed as a husband, leader, and father. I wrote this book to share how these experiences have given me the Leverage To Win time and time again.

I do not claim to have any of the answers to life's tough questions, crises, and trauma we encounter. I want this book to help all who read realize that we share similar needs and we all could use support and someone who will understand. In addition, I would like to use this medium to share my message of hope and help my fellow men find a way to succeed. We were all created for a reason, and in our lifespan, are the key relationships we need to answer the calling and excel in life.

This book is for every person who tries to play life as safe as possible and is ready to train for something better. No one grows in their comfort zone.

Dalton T Beckles

This book is dedicated to my father Dalton T. Beckles Sr.

Introduction

This book is for you. You picked it up and I am grateful you did because it means the world to me. It's also a statement that success means something to you. Whether you want to improve as a father, friend, or leader, this book will aid in your journey to achieve success in multiple areas. You may not know exactly where you want to improve, however, you do know you are ready for a win and I am know this book will provide some clarity. The contents of this book were written to aid in supporting your desire to dream, believe, act, and achieve. It's meant to provide each reader with a foundation of learning skills that will help you in achieving success. *Leverage To Win* reveals the hidden secrets of building achievement by tapping into many of the important relationships in our lives.

I was always afraid of success and thought it was a level in life that was only designed for other people who were not like me. For a long time, I was content going to work, coming home, and staying in my comfort zone every day. At the time, I called this "everyday life" but now, I know it was a conditioned expectation I was following. It was safe, convenient, and for a while, comfortable. I enjoyed coming home, eating whatever I wanted, watching television until I fell asleep, and doing it all over again. To me, that was the life. In some ways, I was happy being able to pay all my bills (barely) and keep up with all the latest Netflix and cable shows. I was comfortable playing Xbox live, yelling at eight-year-old kids, and avoiding my wife who couldn't understand my passion for *Madden* and *Call of Duty*. To me, that's what I worked so hard for.

If you're reading this and you're saying to yourself "yeah, man, that is the life," you might want to put the book down at this point. This book challenges that very lifestyle. During this time whilst binge-watching *Mirrors* on Netflix and downloading the new Ghost Recon on my Xbox, my life hit a new low. Many of my friends began to advance in their careers in ways I didn't in my own career. My best friends who were no longer content living a mediocre life began to break out of the dreaded cycle and started creating success for themselves. One of my closest friends opened a private practice while another friend opened his first physical therapy office.

I felt jealousy grip me like a cramp in my leg and I couldn't shake it. I started to ask myself why I felt frustrated and jealous when comparing the accomplishments of my close friends to my own. I kept wondering why my job no longer met my expectation for success. I was a thirty-four-year-old, overweight, pre-diabetic father on the verge of a divorce, who was no longer excelling in any aspect of life.

I had become so engulfed in my own sorrow and despair my professional work declined to the point of having a promotion rescinded, my marriage was on the rocks, and my weight ballooned to the point I couldn't walk without being tired or in pain. When my French bulldog, Midnight, went missing after a New Year's party, I recognized something had to change in my life and fast if I wanted to make it. As I was writing this book, I realized my life was never designed to turn out this way. I knew I was born with a calling on my life and, to be successful. I also knew God created me for more than what my comfort zone was producing. As we go through the clearly defined steps, you will get some of my life experiences that I used in preparation to be successful, and how I leveraged my own relationships and experiences to turn my life around.

Leverage To Win, is designed to take a closer look at those key characteristics we encounter in our personal relationships and use them to achieve our own success. Often when a change is needed in our lives we don't know where to star or how to break away. We are not sure what steps are needed and fall short on the commitments we have struggled to make. Initially, we are focused and consistent for a while until we start to fall back into unwanted old habits.

Leveraging your natural supports, your experiences, and your community resources are the keys to achieving success at any level. These supports, experiences, and resources are not enough without hard work and persistence. If you want to know what hard work is, then keep reading and apply the understanding of connecting with others who are a clear example of hard work. While I cannot define what success is for you, I do know creating and implementing a plan always equals success. When defining your success, you must be clear, direct, and write down your steps to achievement. Success could be buying your dream home or car, obtaining your dream job, or managing a sustainable income that will provide for your family. Success could be reconnecting with a loved one, writing your first book, starting a blog, a podcast, or getting active in your church. Whatever success is for you, be sure to tap into your supports if you truly want to achieve it. It's what I used when I was down and out and it helped me to achieve several goals I had for myself. I improved my relationship with my wife while also starting my own business and losing close to one hundred pounds. I used my key relationships to build my confidence, and as inspiration and motivation. I have achieved success and continue to achieve more success because I leverage to win. You deserve success and you have all the tools and the key relationships you need to achieve it. As you begin to invest in yourself you will find that the process can be rich and rewarding. You will find that you had the tool to succeed all along. Together we will win.

Section One

Fathers

Chapter 1

I often felt like it was an excuse for most men. You turn on the television, listen to music, or read a book, and hear men and women share how their fathers have impacted their lives. Most men I have encountered in counseling, coaching or just in talking share a story about their father and his impact on their life. The stories aren't very different as it's usually that their father wasn't in their life, or he was only around temporarily, and never developed much of a relationship. I even heard it said once fathers either teach you what to do or, what not to do. It's rare that someone shares a story with me about a father who was always present or, engaging as the leader of the family. Apparently, people don't want to hear about that.

As a nation, we appear to only celebrate overcoming the obstacles of fatherless homes. These obstacles are significant and do provide leverage to overcome challenges, but the part of the story still missing are the positive influences that were present. We will talk about that more when we explore father figures, but it is important to note the role of fathers are impactful. As a kid, all my cousins had both parents in their homes so for me, having a father present in the home was a normal everyday thing. However, many of my closest friends did not have that same experience. I didn't recognize how impactful a relationship with my father was. I didn't see the gift I had that gave me more of an advantage in life. Don't get me wrong, I still grew up poor in the inner city with drugs and violence destroying the community. But my struggle was still easier because of my father's presence. According to the latest research, the lives of children, improve for the better when a father is present, especially in school. Even when fathers do not share a home with their children, their active involvement can have a lasting and positive impact.

While I was doing research for this book, I came across a website dedicated to fathers with a lot of statistics. I found some insightful information that truly rocked me to my core. It was so impactful I called the agency of the Fatherhood Initiative and asked how I could help the organization. The COO of the agency was very pleasant and helpful. Not only did we end up talking about the statistics, but he also sent me a book written by the founder, Ken Canfield (The Heart Of A Father). The book, *The Heart Of A Father,* was a profound read and it motivated me to want to help increase all fathers' participation in their children's lives. The statistics informed me fatherlessness is the most significant family or social problem facing America. The numbers were astounding as it affects so many in childhood through adulthood, over 70.0 %.

I also took some time to read a book on black statistics that also showed people in the African-American community have the highest rate of fatherless homes. This impact in our country is felt in our communities, economy, prison system, and the education field. Further research states *85% of youths in jail currently grew up in a home without a father. Children who grow up in fatherless homes are twice as likely as those with fathers to end up in jail. Those who grow up in a home separate from their father are 4.3 times more likely to be smokers. Children who grew up without a father are twice as likely to drop out of high school, and four times more likely to have emotional or behavioral problems that require assistance. Approximately 75% of teenage suicides occur in a home where one parent is absent. 63% of youth suicides are from fatherless homes. You do the math...if 75% of teenage suicides are where one parent is absent but 63% are from fatherless homes, then only 12% of teenage suicides are from motherless homes. The remaining 25% are from homes with both parents. 15-19-year-old girls that grow up in one-parent homes are far more likely to engage in premarital sex. If a mother attends church regularly with her children but without the father, only 2% will choose to become regular churchgoers as adults. If a father attends church regularly with his children even without the mother, 44% will choose to become regular churchgoers. 75% of young patients seeking substance abuse treatment are from fatherless homes. That's 10 times the average.*

The impact fathers have on our future is pivotal. It's the backbone of our growth and development as a country. Our children, our communities, and our churches need responsible men. That's not to say the world will not continue to strive with women leading it. It simply means we add strength in all areas. The statistics tell a story of the power and strength fathers have on our future and growth as a country and world. Present and active fathers have been on a consistent decline and it's time to change the narrative if we want to succeed. Our success is linked to our relationship with our father and/or a father figure. The importance of fathers is so key to success that I had to address it first in this book. We must acknowledge the magnitude of a father's impact on society. If sons and daughters are not connected too or at least aware of their fathers, then a part of who they are remains undefined and subject to the influence of men around them. Many men are unaware of their father's history, his positive and negative habits and his likes and dislikes. There are traits share by a father's children that could go a long way in making the world a better place. Knowing yourself, your family history and your father aids in you know areas of strength an weakness.

If your biological father was not in your life, it does not mean you did not receive skills necessary for success, or that you are at a disadvantage, or destined to fail. It only means you have an opportunity to develop core values that will sustain you on your journey to success. As we continue through this book, we will talk about father figures, family members, and other important relationships that also provide leverage for you to succeed. If you did have your father in your life, be grateful even if he was not a positive influence.

I believe you can still identify characteristics that you can leverage for success. In the case of the unhealthy father, learn from his mistakes, and do the opposite to achieve success. If your father was abusive, learn to recognize your own emotions and triggers and work to be patient and loving with your own children. If your father was quiet and did not communicate, you must be intentional in your own communication with your children. If your dad didn't spend quality time with you then schedule and plan quality time with your children. Simply do the opposite of what he did and see the benefits. The added value from some simple changes you have experienced in your own life are the added benefit to the healthy growth process of your own children.

You're just like your father! It's a statement that has hurt many young men who either do not have a healthy relationship with their father or who don't know them. The reason for such emotion from such a simple statement is that many young men are striving to be better than their father, and to hear such words can be crushing. Both men and women want more from their fathers.

If this is a statement you have heard before and it stung or made you instantly upset, just know you are not alone. You can see growth and development of our children rely heavily on the relationship with the father. The statistics show the benefits and pitfalls of a father's presence. It also shows a need our country has to build strong and effective leaders. It cannot be ignored. You must use this relationship for leverage if you want to win and achieve success. If you want to be a great father, husband, CEO, leader, speaker or writer then first start with learning from your father.

Chapter 2

My father worked three jobs when I was a kid so I didn't get to spend a lot of time with him. He always wanted to be a full-time marriage and family counselor, and even got a few certificates throughout the years from training and classes he attended, but things never worked out for him. He was always proud of those certificates, and I know he wished he could have done more with them. He would talk so passionately about helping families I could see his love for it. Other priorities prevailed so he put his time and effort into providing for his family. However, my father would still find ways to help in our community, church, and home.

My mother was a housekeeper for most of my childhood while my father worked his many jobs. He started a cleaning business where he would clean doctors' offices throughout New York City. As a kid, I wasn't always happy when he worked so much because I wanted to spend more time with him. That meant I spent a majority of my time with my mother and two sisters. When my father did have free time, he would attempt to spend that time doing something he really enjoyed. He loved playing tennis, soccer, cards, and dominoes with his friends. Every opportunity my father had to go out and enjoy himself he took it, and I remember just watching out of the front window just wishing I could go with him. There were times that he took me with him, friends, and to this day, I still love those moments with my father. Just being around him was better than anything I could imagine.

Many of my friends do not have a story to tell about their father. They either saw their father once, heard about him through family, or met him when they were younger, and stopped having any contact at an early age. The effect this had on them may differ. However, there are some similarities in their development into manhood that may have presented challenges within their own marriages and with their self-esteem.

The idea of being responsible to others, of being leaders in their communities and churches, and even commitment to success has been altered over the years. Men like my father who were once the leaders in their communities have slowly disappeared for various reasons. The task is now left to us as fathers, sons, and husbands to shift the dynamics.

Every summer, my parents would take us kids to Camp Victory Lake in New York. This was a place where all the different Adventist churches in the New York City area would flock to for worship, fun, and a host of activities. My father would load up his van with camping equipment, games, music, his family, and the neighborhood kids who were not a part of our church and haul us up to Camp. The neighborhood kids who came with us always seemed to be having way more fun than we were, and it seemed so weird to me. Here I was the "Church Boy" trying to act cool and act like Camp was so lame while my friends were running, laughing, and enjoying every activity the camp had to offer. When we returned home from camp, all the kids would talk about it the rest of the summer and ask to go with us the following year. While I acted so unhappy about having to go, the kids would be soaking up the attention and care my father gave to them. They craved the attention and excitement he showed when they would run fast, catching the ball, or not get tagged while running the bases. They enjoyed having someone be proud of them. A man like my father who took the time to nurture a group of boys who at the time didn't get that very often. After growing up in the inner city surrounded by violence, drug addiction, and poverty, it felt good getting away from the everyday cycle of life. What I thought would be so "not cool" was a breath of fresh air. These kids would hang onto every word my father spoke, and never complained or argued. When he would ask someone to pray or read from the Bible, they jumped at the opportunity. I didn't understand it at all. I was embarrassed my father was talking about God or reading the Bible. But they were just happy to have a man show interest in them. It took me many years to truly appreciate my father and all the wisdom he attempted to bestow upon me. He would sit me down after trips and tell me a man must take care of his family no matter how he felt about it. He would tell me that we are called to help others, and that a real man does not harm others. I will never forget when he told me true strength is not defined by hurting someone but by knowing you can hurt someone and choosing not to. That statement has stuck with me to this day. I know I am strong, I know there are people out there who mean us harm and ill will. But I also know that hurting them does not make me a man or a better person. What makes me a man is doing the right thing even when it's not easy to do. My father did not talk much, but when he spoke it was deep, thoughtful, and impactful. By the time I was in college, I found myself missing and craving my father. And just like the great man he is, he tailored his life to fit mine when I needed him.

When I was thirteen years old, my father decided to move us out of New York to live in Sterling VA. To me, this was the worst thing that could happen to an adolescent boy. On the first day of school, I was riding the bus when I met a wild and full-of-energy character named Kevyn. He was everything I wasn't. Confident, handsome and funny. Kevyn was a class clown and made every day of eighth-grade-year fun until he, his mom and his little brother moved away. His mother was getting married and moving in with her future husband. I rarely saw Kevyn much over the next year but we stayed in contact by phone.

By the tenth grade, Kevyn had a girlfriend with a car so she would take him wherever he wanted to go, which meant we got to hang out, play ball, and talk about girls. Kevyn became my closest friend and even came to stay on some weekends. One day, my father got a call from Kevyn's mother. Kevyn had been kicked out of another school and she said she had had enough. She told my father Kevyn was not listening, and he refused to follow any rules at all. When I got home from work that evening, my father told me about the phone call and asked me to pick Kevyn up.

When I got to the house, Kevyn was sitting in his room with tears in his eyes and his bags packed. I asked him what was going on, and after a moment of silence, he said, "she's getting married again." I couldn't understand the complexity of the statement, but I could see the pain in his eyes. Kevyn, the funny, full-of-energy kid I knew was now a tearful, depressed, and frustrated boy. He didn't have a relationship with his father and he watched his mother go from man to man, being treated terribly by these men who had no intention of being a father figure. Kevyn was silent the entire ride back to my house and I didn't bother him. The rest of the week, Kevyn stayed with us while my father tried to figure out what to do next. Eventually, he had a conversation with Kevyn asking if he wanted to stay with us for a while. Kevyn lowered his head and stated he would like that very much.

My father spent the next few weeks, working on becoming Kevyn's guardian, getting him into school, and getting him a job. Under the leadership of my father's directions, Kevyn's entire life began to change. Although school was always a challenge for Kevyn, he began to excel at his after-school job, and was even promoted to shift manager at the local restaurant before his seventeenth birthday. He attended church with us and spent time with my father prepping and preparing for his future. The power of a father figure can make a big difference in how we turn out as men. While we all may not have a father in our lives, it is very important to have a father figure who you can look up to for guidance and direction. It doesn't matter your age, you're never too old to learn and model the actions of a father figure.

A father figure may have to make sacrifices to improve the lives of others. While as a kid my father made sure he made time for himself, he also started to invest in things I liked as well. My father is a homegrown West Indian who enjoys, cricket, tennis, and soccer. However, I am a New Yorker who loved playing basketball and watching the Knicks. My father would come out to the basketball court and play his heart out just to spend time with me. Crazy thing is that although he sucked, it meant the entire world to me. He would take me to Knicks vs Wizards games and also pay for me to bring friends. That's what a father does and that's why they are needed. They grow us and teach so much by leading and being the example. So, what do we do when Dad isn't around? We identify a father figure. Someone who has taken the time to show us a better way in life. As men, we need to be responsible and dependable. We must return to our homes, our churches, and our communities. Because, without a father or a father figure's leadership, all mentioned areas will continue to suffer and disappear.

My father understood this concept very well. He understood the importance of sacrifice and demonstrated for me the importance of it as I struggled in college. I will never forget how every year, starting with my junior year in college until I moved out of Michigan, my father would take his annual vacation time and spend one full week with me. As an adult, I asked him why he would spend his vacation in boring old Michigan with me instead of going away with mom or going to Trinidad. He simply stated he wanted to ensure my success. My father's success was in ensuring my success. True success is in encouraging and supporting the success of others. If you want to be successful, be mindful to ensure the success of others. Becoming a giver is the greatest reward. A major reason so many men fail is because their focus is on what they can get rather than what they can give. He has always been a giver and he has been rewarded for his giving ways. As I reflect on my relationship with my father, I can point out examples of how the influence of my father led to my personal success.

My father displayed kindness and patience with everyone he encountered which is a characteristic I carry with me in my own life. I learned by his actions to listen and help others and, as a result, I excelled as a social worker. He allowed his actions to speak for him in everything he did. He did not do a lot of talking; he would rather work and follow through on his word. When I need to buckle down, I do the same in my own life and instead of talking about things I allow my actions to speak for me. He was determined to provide for his family at any cost as evidenced by working up to three jobs at a time. His work ethic was phenomenal and a valued asset. He also made his decisions based on the needs of his family. If you want to be successful as a father, I suggest you learn this and implement it in your life.

My father didn't let other people bring him down. While he was not a very educated man by today's standards, he never allowed someone else to determine his worth. He loved my mother unconditionally. His love and passion for his family goes beyond the norm of what even I can comprehend. He never raised his hand or his voice towards my mother, and was always respectful and loving. Of course, they had disagreements but never would my father become verbally or physically aggressive. He treated both my mother and sisters with the utmost respect. It's a characteristic I try to emulate every day with my family. Lastly, my father never gave up. Whatever he put his mind to achieve, he did. If he wanted a specific job, he would work tirelessly to get to that position. He wouldn't let anything stop him from achieving his goal.

When our family moved to Virginia, my father got a part-time job as a guest service agent (bell boy) at a well-known resort in Leesburg VA. As you can imagine, the job was employed by young men who were nearly twenty years younger than my father. The resort where my father worked was well-known as a place many rich and famous people would stay. My father met Charles Barkley, Bill Russell,

Colin Powell, George Bush Sr. and host of other people during his time as a guest service agent. Even though he was twice the age of the other staff, my father worked tirelessly and had the tips to show for it. His bosses saw his work ethic and invested in him. In a matter of months, he was promoted to a night auditing position within the hotel. He worked the new position for about eighteen months and worked his way up to Night Resort Manager. His work ethic has always been inspiring to me and I put forth the same effort when I work as a Clinical Director and as I work for myself as an entrepreneur. Seeing what my father accomplished in his life with limited education, low wages and four mouths to feed is what I now use as leverage to win. My father taught me that a good work ethic and consistency were keys to success. He worked consistently and always gave his best to his family, community, and church. And even as an adolescent boy who wished for more time with my dad, I always admired his ability to be superman in our family.

My father is now retired and enjoying his time with my mother. He still volunteers at his church and is pursuing a new goal as a lay preacher. For many of the men and women my father has worked with as Pathfinder director, counselor and father figure, his impact on their lives are still felt to this day. There are many places I go to speak where I am recognized as Dalton's son. I then listen as many people share their stories with me of how my father impacted their lives. That's leverage to win.

Chapter 3

We already addressed the fact that fathers are important and father figures are just as important. It is one thing for a biological father to take responsibility for their children. However, for a man who is not a biological father to take on such a responsibility for a child makes the connection is a blessing and a gift. I myself had great father figures in my life. My grandfather (my dad's father) was the kindest man I know. I could clearly see where my father got a lot of his character from. My grandfather passed away in 2014 from cancer and at his funeral, you could see the legacy he left behind. You could see the lives he touched and the impact he made. My grandfather moved his entire family from the beautiful island of Trinidad to New York City for a better life. My grandfather worked hard and opened his home to all his family throughout the years. When he retired, he allowed his children to live in his house while he and my grandmother moved into affordable housing. When he moved to Florida, he let my cousin move into his apartment at the same affordable rate. My grandfather did not have much, but what he had he gave to his family. My grandfather also gave to all of his grandchildren. He would give us envelopes of money at Christmas time and take us shopping at Toys r Us for our birthdays. I do not know a person kinder than my grandfather who always gave but didn't ask for anything in return.

As I watched people's reaction during the service, I was overwhelmed by how many people were there to pay respect. It wasn't just family, but friends, neighbors, and old coworkers who made the trip from Trinidad, New York, and Maryland. I listened to their stories, I watched their tears roll, and I got emotional just thinking about how loved he was by everyone.

When the program started and they began to read his obituary, I broke down in tears. It was the first time in my life I learned we shared the same middle name. Learning this information created a whole new connection to my grandfather because no one else had his name but my father. That made me feel so special knowing I was left to carry on his legacy. It also showed me the respect my father had for his father to give me the name his father gave him. It's my hope that if I am blessed to have a son, I will also be able to give him the name Theophilous. (Lover of God). Family legacy and a name alone will give you leverage to win.

When I was getting ready to enter high school, my mother decided to send me to stay with one of her brothers in Staten Island NY for a few weeks. We had just moved to Virginia and things were not going well for me. My mother was at a loss with what to do with me, so she reached out to my uncle and he agreed to take me for a while. I was not happy about this. My uncle was an older man with children much older than me. He was an accountant with his own business in Manhattan. As a kid growing up in Queens, my parents would take us to visit my uncle at his job in Manhattan and, to me, it was boring. I would sit on the chair and dream I was anywhere else but there. The entire ride to his home in Staten Island from Virginia was torture.

The trip started off with him praying, which just made me roll my eyes. It was followed up with books on tape, news radio, and political conversations. I couldn't help but think how horrible this trip would be. How could my mother think this was a good idea? My uncle and I didn't have anything in common. He was a very spiritual man who was well-educated and in my eyes boring. It felt like a punishment, and while I wanted to be in NY for the summer, I did not want to spend my time between Staten Island and Manhattan sitting in an accountant's office. Once we arrived on Staten Island and got in the car, he prayed again thanking Yahweh for everything and then we drove to his home. At his home, I said hello to his wife and he showed me to my room. I remember sitting on the bed and really hoping that someone would rescue me from bondage. When no one came to rescue me, I decided to try to make the best of my situation.

My uncle was sitting on the couch catching up on soccer highlights and score updates on sports center. He had his wife record the soccer games and he asked if I wanted to watch. I told him soccer wasn't my sport but I would check it out. He asked me what sport I liked and I told him that I liked basketball. He smiled and asked me which basketball team did I like, to which I responded the Knicks. My uncle smirked as most people do when I mention my favorite basketball team, but then my uncle said, "Hmm, interesting, I know Patrick very well." I said you know who? My uncle told me he used to work with some of the Knick players like Patrick Ewing and John Starks. In an instant, my mood and attitude shifted! I was now in awe of my uncle. I said to myself, how the heck did you pull that off. My uncle spoke so nonchalantly about these players as if they were just regular guys. He told me that he did their taxes but he wasn't a big fan of the team. I was in shock... My boring, educated, professor of an uncle was a fan of basketball? Of the Knicks? He may not have known it then, but in that moment, he became the coolest person on the planet to me. I probably asked him fifty more questions throughout the night. I went to bed that night with my uncle and the Knicks on my mind.

The next day when we arrived at the office, my uncle took me to a backroom filled with files and tons of boxes. He asked me to come and help him go through some of the boxes before he started work. I opened a box and had the hugest grin on my face. It was a box full of basketball cards, jet magazines, and basketball magazines. My uncle told me I could go through the boxes and read anything that I wanted to. I spent the next two weeks going through every magazine and basketball cards I could get my hands on. There was never a dull moment. When he had a free moment, he would come to the backroom to check on me, and answer any questions I had. He just stood there smiling and said, "Man, you really like the Knicks." I responded with a resounding yes! And began to tell him all about my love for John Starks, Patrick Ewing, Charles Oakley, and Anthony Mason. One evening, my uncle came into my room because he wanted to share something with me. He took me to a closet in which was filled with VHS tapes. He told me that I could look through the VHS tapes and watch anything I wanted. Inside this closet was every playoff game the Knicks had played dating back to 1991.

If I wasn't in love with my uncle before, I was now. I watched every game I could until it was time to go back home to Virginia. I asked him basketball questions, work-related questions, and even about his achievements. My uncle was always very humble and gave all the glory to God for what he had received. He told me hard work and kindness, are so important if I wanted to make something of myself. His lessons had so much meaning because I was able to see my uncle in a different light.

While I did not want to be an accountant, being around my uncle made me want to adopt many of his principals and characteristics. I wanted the success my uncle had and I also wanted to be able to attend Knicks games when I wanted. I slowly began to validate and appreciate my uncle in a way he could not imagine. I began to admire his work ethic and passion for life. I started to see more than just a man but a leader. My uncle accomplished so much in his career while still finding time to enjoy his hobbies and family. I wanted to learn as much as I could from him so that someday, I could also enjoy the spoils of life. I wanted to enjoy living in a nice home with a nice car, buying whatever I wanted to buy and getting courtside seats to Knicks games. He inspired me to want better for myself. That's the power of a father figure. In positive or negative, father figures inspire us to want more. I saw so many of my neighborhood and school friends flock to the corner where many of the drug dealers and gang members were because that's where the father figures were. A huge responsibility had been placed on our church men/pastors/elders, coaches and community center workers. I saw it firsthand. I understand its importance and I hope you too now see.

Fathers and father figures play a key role in the success of every man. One of the greatest joys of my life was becoming a father. When I heard my daughter's heartbeat for the first time, I was moved with so much emotion I couldn't even contain it. Tears poured down my face as I began to dream of my life with my child. When she born, I was scared and excited all at once. This beautiful gift that I was holding in my arms was so amazing and she didn't even know it or understand it. The impact my daughter had on my life was instant and life-changing. Being a father has done more for me and my own success than I could have ever imagined. Being around someone who thinks the world of you and sees you as a superhero builds so much confidence. Wanting to give the world to her was life-changing. Some people look at children as a burden and goal sacrifice. For me, it presented an opportunity and provided motivation. I wanted to give my daughter a better life, and I also want to be her hero always. That meant that changes had to be made. Though I did not move right away as my wife will tell you, I started to list my priorities and plan for my future. Although I didn't start off as a great father, I did start to dream. And as we will discuss later in the book, learning to dream and dream big leads to action and growth.

As we close this section, we discussed fathers and father figures. Please be sure to identify both entities in your life and create a list of gifts and attributes they both hold and what characteristics you can leverage to win in life. Keep in mind that anyone who takes the time to teach, support and ensure your success can be put in the category of a father figure. In order to leverage this relationship to win, you must identify the characteristics and lessons they shared with you in your life. When you think about your goals and the areas you want to obtain success in, you must answer what your father and father figures can share that will give you that leverage.

Section 2

Brotherhood

Chapter 4

Brotherhood is a big deal for many men. I want to make sure we pay close attention to this section. It's important to pay attention because this is the first area in which you (the reader) make or made friendship choices that may have a huge impact on your success. In the previous section, we discussed fathers and father figures and their impact. For the most part, you didn't pick your father or father figure. But you did and do get to pick your friends and who you associate yourself with. Your brothers will have a huge impact on your personal and professional life. You didn't get to pick your teachers, or your family members, but you did pick your brothers. It is so important to choose wisely who you decide to call brother. I cannot stress how important this is. Your brothers have a big influence in your life as they offer advice, push you to do great things or push you in the wrong direction. In this section, I want to share with you how some of the friends and family members I call brothers have pushed me towards success. As we go through this section, please identify those close males who you call brother. It's important because these men in some way have played a role in how you currently view the world. Their opinion on women, money, society, and spirituality tend to play a role in how you view those same areas. We want to connect with others who share similar beliefs as our own or we pretend to share in their beliefs until we actually do. When we start to pretend, we end up becoming something that we never intended to become. We end up not being our best as fathers, friends, husbands, or leaders. We spend our time either continuing to try to fit in with the status quo or end up losing out on some amazing opportunities. Our marriages end in divorce, our careers hit a rut, and we sit depressed and overweight wondering where we went wrong. We end up stuck living a conditioned life working for someone who stayed true to themselves and followed their calling. As I mentioned previously, we all have a calling on our lives, and when we pretend to be something that we are not, we end up living a nightmare. Having the right people around you, your brothers who can hold you accountable and support you as your true self is beneficial when looking for leverage to win. Brothers who can laugh at you, compete with you and pray with you. Brothers who bring your gifts and talents to the next level. In this section, we will explore some of my brothers who have given me leverage to win.

If the people that you have around you do not appear to support your dreams or push you to greatness then I feel comfortable telling you to find different friends as soon as possible. If your brothers cannot be honest with you then I would not consider them a brother. A true brother is someone who will lift you up and support your calling in life. Let's dig in and see if we can identify some real brothers like I did.

Chapter 5

Throughout the years, I have been blessed to have many close friendships. As a kid growing up in New York, I had my close friend, Gabe, who is also my oldest friend. We did everything together as kids. We played basketball and swam at the rec center, went to the same church, and spent weekends at each other's house. I cannot tell you how or when I met Gabe. I only remember that we were always close friends that met at church. Gabe was always confident and fearless. It's a trait I always admired about him and made me want to hang with him all the time. While I was timid and soft, Gabe was the complete opposite in public. Gabe was confident and strong, always fighting older kids, doing tricks on his bike, and getting into trouble at school and church. I always leveraged Gabe's confidence to try new things as a kid and in college. When I tried out for the basketball team, I only did it because Gabe said he would do it with me. I was asked to join a drama club in college; once again, I only did it because Gabe said he would do it with me.

The summer before I moved to Virginia solidified my friendship with Gabe. To the outside world, Gabe was a courageous and adventurous kid. He was always in trouble, got into fights, and had a reputation for being a daredevil, but the Gabe I knew was quite different. One day, we were driving back from a party in Long Island with Gabe's dad when the engine died on the highway. Gabe and I were sitting in the back seat just laughing and talking when the car started to sputter and slow to a complete stop. Gabe's dad was able to maneuver the car to the side of the road without causing an accident and then he set out to find a pay phone to call for help. Now this was back in 1993, so there weren't any cell phones at the time. Gabe's dad left us with the car and told us he would be back with help. We stayed in that car for what must have been six hours. With all that time on our hands and nothing to do, we spent the next few hours talking. To this day, I am grateful for that trip. Gabe and I talked about everything going on in our lives and we really opened up to each other. This is significant because it is rare that males open up at any age and share their thoughts, fears, and feelings. Gabe and I shared it all, and this car ride, stuck on the side of the highway bonded us for life.

This car ride taught me that people don't always express their true feelings unless they feel safe and comfortable. I had known Gabe for most of my life and it took us being stranded on the highway to truly share our thoughts on a deeper level. Because of this interaction, I had an outlet as a kid that most males don't have. I now had a friend who I could be myself around and share my thoughts. As a kid, I was afraid to talk to girls, but I couldn't tell anyone that because it wasn't cool. Having a friend like Gabe allowed me to express it and not feel embarrassed. Gabe just looked at me and told me he was scared too. A brotherhood was born that day that carries on till today.

Learning to leverage your personal relationships to achieve goals is important to recognize as children as well as adults. When my family moved out of New York City, I was worried about how I would adjust without Gabe. Although I leveraged the relationship, I didn't learn how to use it to build my own confidence. My confidence was still dependent on Gabe being by my side. That same confidence transferred to Kevyn who became that person for me. It wasn't until I was in college and Gabe left to study abroad that I learned to have my own identity. In high school, I had my friends Jomo, Kevyn, and Carlos. We played ball together, listened to music and talked to girls. I am still in contact with all of my friends, and I call these guys my brothers. Each of my friends will tell you the influence we all had on each other were positive and beneficial. We created a bond with each other that allowed us to speak openly and freely with each other. We didn't have to pretend or act tough with each other, we could be ourselves. We fought like brothers, attended Knicks Vs Wizards games, shared sneakers, basketball jerseys, and food. We even all worked together at a local restaurant called Chicken Out. Even though I started working at an early age, working with my friends was a different experience. You could tell we pushed each other because we didn't goof off at work. We worked hard and pushed each other to excel. I honestly thought I would still be working there managing several of the stores until my mom dashed that dream. My friends were hard workers and each of us are better for it. Through this opportunity, we were able to see our gifts and the potential for more. We all went to different colleges but stayed in contact and supported each other as best we could.

These relationships truly helped us to make it through those difficult adolescent years when it felt like the world was against us. While these friendships were very important during this time it was just a stepping stone for something greater. As much as I want to go more into this subject, this book isn't about this phase of my life. I took some time to talk about it because it's important to recognize who you have around you at an early age. Because life doesn't always afford us a clean perfect hand we have to be intentional about who we let in our circle. I was lucky when I look back at my friends but everyone isn't so lucky. My brothers didn't pressure me to drink, smoke, or cut school. I picked a group of friends who were down to earth and fit my personality well. Once Keyvn left high school, I spent most of my time with Carlos. Carlos was into hip-hop and we spent a lot of time at his house listening to records. He also lived one block away from the basketball courts so his house was the hangout spot for Jomo and I. The three of us would hang out rapping and eating his parents out of house and land and then go to the park to shoot hoops. Neither Carlos nor Jomo had brothers so we became brothers to each other and hung out all the time. Each of us could have chosen to hang out with other people, but we all connected through our love of music and the freedom we shared to be ourselves. Growing up in New York, I felt a lot of pressure to be something that I wasn't. I felt pressure to act tough in order not to be picked on or bullied. In school, I acted as the class clown which got me kicked out of class daily and caused my grades to suffer. I acted as a clown because in school I wasn't tough and being a clown also made the tough guys like you and not bother you. In Virginia, I didn't have to act tough or be a clown. Carlos and Jomo did not care about that. They were more concerned about who was better, Biggie or Tupac. They were concerned about just being kids. My parents moving the family may have been one of the best decisions ever made for my own future success. Although I had a great friend in Gabe, the

"Friends" I associated myself with in Queens were not making me a better person. By the age of thirteen, I was failing my classes and needed to repeat the seventh grade.

I was getting kicked out of class every week and hanging with some of the boys in my neighborhood who had already quit going to school. My choices at the time were just plain stupid. Many of you who are reading this book may be feeling like you are or were living in similar communities where the options for positive influences were limited. You will have to be intentional about finding people who share your passions and allow you to be yourself without having to pretend to be someone else. Once the pressure was taken off of me to be something I wasn't, I could be myself. My grades improved and I never again got kicked out of class or failed a class. During my first semester in Virginia, I got straight A's and was returned to my right grade in the middle of my second semester.

Chapter 6

During my adolescent years when I was most impressionable, I had two close family members who were like brothers to me and left a major imprint on my life. My closest male family members were my cousins, Samuel and Cordelle. Samuel was my older cousin on my mother's side of the family and the son of one of my father figures. Cordelle was my cousin on my father's side and the closest thing I will ever have to an actual brother. The relationships I built with both men have been nothing shorter than a blessing in my life. Samuel being significantly older than me was more of a mentor than a brother. He was very active in church and always made me feel like I was the most important person in the world. His demeanor and confidence are traits to be desired by any young man.

Cordelle also being the only boy in his family with two sisters treated me like his little brother. Sam would take me on outings as a kid to basketball and baseball games, and Cordelle and I would work on bikes, hang out and run the streets and just be kids. With my father working as much as he did, and no other males in the home, I began to crave more and more time with both of my cousins. Neither seemed to mind having me around and never once did I hear either of them complain about anything. As Sam got older and got married, I began to spend more time with Cordelle and really took a liking to his character and demeanor. Cordelle was always kind and never appeared to let anything upset him or get him down. He was laid back, calm, cool and collected. But most of all, Cordelle was respectful and kind.

I was in church every weekend hanging with Gabe, but I never knew Cordelle to go to church. Yet Cordelle was much more of Christian than me. By the time we were teenagers, with Cordelle being about three years older than me, he was doing a better job of showing me what a Christian was than I was showing him. One day, we had just finished playing basketball at the park in Rochdale Village in Queens, a housing project, when we started walking back to the apartment building were Cordelle was living. We saw a woman walking back from the grocery store carrying several bags on her own. She was walking ahead of us, but you could tell she was struggling to carry the bags. When we caught up with her, Cordelle stopped and asked the lady if he could help her with the bags. She said thank you and accepted the help. Cordelle passed me a few bags and took the other bags from the lady and we walked her to her apartment and left without saying a word. Cordelle and I never talked about the situation, but I remember thinking to myself the entire time that in church we are taught to help others and my cousin who had never been to church acted instinctively without that same education. This wouldn't be the last time that a similar situation would occur and my admiration and appreciation for Cordelle continued to grow and made me want to be that kind of person who helped people without hesitation. In a time when most young men were looking to join gangs, prove how manly they were, Cordelle was more concerned with playing football, meeting girls and hanging with his friends in the neighborhood. Although I was younger, they still let me hang out with them and kept me out of trouble. To this day, he's still close with his friends and even created a business with them remodeling homes.

These small but significant experiences I share with my cousins have shaped the kind of person I would become. I learned to be kind and patient with people and supportive of their goals and dreams. I learned to be kind to strangers and treat people with love and respect because my cousin showed me that it was good to do. Cordelle could have walked past that lady and I would have learned it was "OK" to do. His decision to help made me feel more confident to do the right thing even at an age when most teenage boys were causing trouble. To this day, Cordelle and I are still close and I have yet to hear him complain about anything. He continues to work hard and provide the best life for his wife and children. Cordelle was a perfect brother at a critical time in my life where we shape and form copies of who we think we want to be.

Chapter 7

If you want to be successful then I suggest you pick your friends very wisely and take advantage of the opportunities to learn and develop new skills. One of the smartest decisions I ever made was picking a great group of friends to call my brothers. I joined a Christian organization while in college, and at the time, I didn't recognize the true gift that it was. I can firmly state that I am successful now because of the many lessons learned while apart of this organization. Some of the young men I met in this organization have genuinely become my brothers. These guys opened my eyes to my true potential and pushed me to strive for more. We have been in each other's life since meeting in the early 2000s and continue to push and challenge each other for the better.

While I have a very close bond with many members of our brother and sisterhood, I'd like to highlight some specific members who went the extra mile in leading the organization. These members all seemed destined for success and we supported each other every chance we got. Each of us bringing our talents, gifts, and skills we learned back at home to the table whenever we met. I can honestly say that their influence in my life is paramount. These guys exemplify the idea of taking skills learned in their upbringing, gleaning knowledge from mother and father figures and taking passion, drive, and persistence to achieve success. They pushed me in ways most young men wouldn't. They are all leaders in their churches, fathers or father figures in their homes, and active members in their communities. When you find men, who display these kinds of characteristics, you should be intentional about connecting with them. Even as an eighteen-year-old boy, they connected with me and saw my potential. A sure fact that you were meant for greatness is when others see that greatness in you. My brothers saw that in me and I saw it in them too. It became almost a healthy competition to push for more and more. College allowed us the opportunity to try new things and tap into our creative side.

When I got to college, my passion shifted from basketball to music. I was involved with other campus activities but music had taken over my life. I was writing, recording and producing morning, noon and night. I was nervous to do anything on my own at that age, but when another group of guys invited me to record in their dorm room, I seized the opportunity. After I recorded my verse, I started craving to record more and more. But I didn't know much about the recording process and I had no equipment of my own. Unsure of what to do, I started recording on an old computer I had with a computer mic. It sounded terrible but I enjoyed it and kept going. I found myself at the computer writing and recording for hours to the point where I looked up and realized I had missed almost a week of classes. I told myself I was just going to quit school and focus on music full-time. I would become a rapper! I called my mom to give her the good news and she simply told me that I was going to do no such thing.

Although my dreams of becoming a famous rapper died before they ever truly started, I didn't stop rapping right away and, my brothers are the reason why I didn't stop. My brothers encouraged me to pursue my passion and focus in school simultaneously. They started hanging out in my dorm room making sure I attended class and even tried their hand at rapping with me. We started getting into a pattern of working hard at the beginning of each week, and by the weekend, we were cutting loose. My brothers were also very involved in school activities, church, and committed relationships. I will admit that by today's standards my brothers are a rare breed. We all had our war stories of trauma and family issues we had endured in our lives, however, we had a passion in us that needed to be fed and connected us. As adults, we continue to support and push each other to achieve success. We check in monthly and review our personal and professional goals. We support each other in business endeavors, weight loss, and goal setting accountability. Several of my brothers are also entrepreneurs who have their own businesses and do well for themselves. It makes things easier when you are surrounded by other smart and educated businessmen that you can also call brothers.

Chapter 8

In the current times we live in, it may not be as easy to find a group of men who will pray with you, push you educationally and show you how to treat a woman. Men who are able to see a future better than the current life they live. It's as if being a positive influence on others, doing things in a legal and positive way are looked down upon as a negative thing. Yet the men who go against this negative type of thinking will have a higher chance of success.

Some who read this chapter may think this is soft or weird, however, I urge you to look at some of the most successful and positive men you know now and think about what they did in order to get to where they are. Jay Z changed his friends often and quickly to achieve his success. If his friends/brothers were not trying to attain more in life, he wanted nothing to do with them. But let's think smaller than that, think about that boy or girl in your school that is or was always involved in activities, that didn't care about parties or gossip but was focused on taking advantage of all there was to offer. While you thought they were weird (unless that person was you), they were taking advantage of the opportunities that you may have taken for granted.

My brothers were not perfect at all and made many mistakes. We were not intentional about securing our futures or building on our talents, gifts or passion. We were just your everyday guys who liked to play cards, basketball, hang with our girlfriends and we have a lot of fun. Had we been intentional about planning for our future, some of the success we see in other people would have been ours at an earlier age. One thing we did have is a good balance between having fun and educational development. Because we all felt free to be ourselves we did not have to act hard or pretend to be something we weren't. While other guys were failing classes, getting kicked out of school, and losing scholarships, we were excelling in the classroom and with campus activities. Looking back on my life at that time, I wish that we had been more intentional about improving our talents and building a brand rather than just having fun. That's another nugget of this book! The people who are most successful are those who take advantage of the opportunities provided. My brothers and I had so many opportunities, and while we did use our gifts, we didn't use them intentionally with a goal of maximizing our potential which is important.

Many young men who lived or are living in disadvantaged situations may feel as though they have not been given a fair opportunity which may be true. Life has not always afforded us the close friendships, father, and mother figures capable of teaching us the skills we need for success. That's why I wrote this book, to encourage you to tap into natural resources that can still produce skills for success. Just because your father was not at home does not mean you cannot be a great father. If I asked what made you most upset about your father growing up, many would maybe say that their father not being around or promising to visit but never showing up would be their answer. So, just being in your child's life is a success! Just show up consistently could be enough to change the narrative for your child. As you're reading, you may also be thinking about the family around you that isn't supportive. You see the friends in your neighborhood and school and feel like they are not trying to do anything with their life. Don't be discouraged. Be intentional. Connect with the people who are trying to do something with their life. Yes, you have to battle some fear and discouragement, yes, you will have the history of your family to contend with, but that's all mental. That's a mental challenge that you must defeat. But one thing I know for sure is that faith trumps fear any day of the week!

The stories we hear of successful men may speak of how to work hard and persevere through tons of adversity which don't always seem lucrative or appealing to the everyday man. But I believe that being intentional about who we choose to call brothers plays a major role. If we glean knowledge from our supports, build a relationship with God, utilize our gifts, talents, and passions then success will come.

Chapter 9

Ollege was the first time I chose to tap into my gifts on my own. It felt more like exploration and creativity, but that's when the foundations of who I would become were forming. One of my brothers, now a well-known author and speaker, reached out to me about putting together a six-week seminar on campus for women and men. His idea was that we would meet with men and women weekly to talk about wellness, hope, and self-improvement. We offered this seminar to our fellow classmates for free and we had huge turnouts. Each week, we would meet, prepared with PowerPoint presentations, handouts, and engaging topics that left each person in attendance coming back each week. While my brother could have asked many other people to work on such an awesome seminar, I like to believe he saw potential in me. Seeing my own potential was not always an easy task. It would be a major issue for me and for anyone else who is not always able to see their value. I enjoyed doing the seminar so much that when I graduated from college, I added it to my resume and sought out opportunities to train and speak in public about topics I was knowledgeable in. This brings me to my first point. 1. Surround yourself with people who believe in you and see your true potential.

There was another time while in grad school that I started to work with some of the younger guys in school on music. Because music was such a passion for me, I wanted to share it and help others who showed that same passion. I started a group called diverse minds with a young kid from Detroit and another kid from Florida. I was determined that with their skills, we could really do something special and share our music with the world. During the summer break with both guys back at their family homes, I started the process of putting together a recording space and working on obtaining the needed equipment. Once again, my brother who I worked with on the seminar saw the potential in my vision and literally spent the next month helping me build a studio inside of the apartment. There was no benefit for him except he saw my potential and the impact it would have on others around me.

Point number two. When a creative idea hits you, take full advantage of it and figure out the rest later. Although I did not have all the answers, others saw my vision and helped me to turn that dream into a reality. Just so you know, both of those guys from diverse minds have gone on to do some amazing things. One of them received several stellar award nominations for his music production and had an opportunity to work with Lecrae, a major recording hip-hop artist. The other guy started his own business and, in turn, helped me build and grow my own business. When opportunities are created, it opens the door for you to dream and explore your passion.

Opportunities always seem to arise in your life when you are working in your calling. It is not only through your calling that opportunities are created but, it is the most effective because you are prepared for it. My passions and my calling have been two separate things for me. Often, we try to combine the two which can prove disastrous. Your passion can lead to your calling but your calling may not be your passion. I loved rapping and I loved playing basketball but I never felt like it was my calling in life. My passion for music and basketball did aid me in my calling. It helped me to learn to listen and work with a team. It helped me to understand the importance of playing a specific role for the benefit of a team. However, being passionate or having a passion for something does not make me talented at doing it myself. Your calling on the other hand, it's seen by not only yourself but the people around you. You may have heard it before if someone told you that you were really good at something and that you should be doing this all the time. You may not be passionate about it, but it's still your calling. You have a gift in that area and the people around you will encourage you to pursue it.

When I entered graduate school to work on my social work degree, I was fortunate to have another male in my class. During undergrad, my friend Adrian and I ran in different circles, but in graduate school we grew much closer due to having many of the same classes and shared internships. During undergrad, Adrian also tried his hand at rapping and we actually met by working on a few songs together. He wasn't a social work major at the time so we would only really talk if we were working on a song. When I was finally ready to get my act together educationally, I was worried about going for my masters without the support of my previous advisor, Michael Wright. I was already warned that I would have to maintain a high GPA if I wanted to complete my degree in less than two years and I knew I did not like research. I was praying for a miracle when Adrian walked into the classroom and sat right next to me. Over the next two years, Adrian and I attended class, internships and completed projects together. This was so helpful because it set the stage for both of us to win in school. We helped each other with assignments, we joked about everything and we created our own internship in Indiana sharing our love of music and therapy. When I graduated with my degree, I got a job in Michigan, and when Adrian graduated, I was able to get him a job at the same agency. For the next five years, our friendship continued to grow as Adrian and I worked together as social workers, played basketball in the summer league we started and talked about life as men while playing madden on Xbox. Adrian and I share a lot of similarities in the career paths we choose, however, Adrian was someone who had already learned to leverage his relationships to succeed. Adrian had his own group of friends during college and graduate school but Adrian also seemed to manage himself effectively. His connection to God was strong and there was never a question of his faith. I admired his confidence and faithfulness to his wife and would often find myself talking to him about life, love and faith. With his great sense of humor, Adrian helped me the most when I was thinking about asking my wife to marry me. I won't go into the details of the conversation but I will say that Adrian helped to put things into perspective for me when I struggled. Friendships like Adrian's are not to be forgotten or taken for granted. When tasked with a difficult decision, I often ask myself, what would Adrian do? It's important to connect with friends that are positive and that share similar passions. Connect with other men that have a connection to God and that are also excellent examples of what respect and loyalty look like. Adrian, if you read this, I thank you for helping me and giving me leverage to win. Your ability to share your gifts and talents created the path for you to step out on faith and impact my life as well as many others on the way to your own success. Adrian Currently resides in Illinois with his lovely wife and two beautiful children. He continues to share his talents and works as a therapist in the Chicago area.

Chapter 10

When I think back to my most creative opportunities in college where I showed initiative, three specific opportunities come to mind. My Thoughts/Team Gully, Summer Basketball League and The Master's talk radio. Each significant for different reasons but all with the underlying fact of me tapping into my passion and potential. Although afraid to lead on my own, I still call them placeholders to leading to the man I would become once on my own.

You read earlier about my love for music. Well, it was a love that I wanted to share with the world. But not just my music but another artist too. I wanted to take the campus by storm and get all the talented artists involved. As you know, my brother saw my vision and helped me to build a studio. But there was more to the story, prior to this, my brothers saw me working hard on my craft every day. They saw me writing, rehearsing, and recording all the time. I entitled my projects "My Thoughts" because the music was therapy for me and I was just sharing my thoughts. I worked so hard that the running joke was that I had tons of my thoughts albums hidden away like Tupac. My brothers helped to promote my music on campus as well as in the community and even organized an Album release party for me. We had no idea what we were doing but we put our best foot forward and had a great time doing it. I even got my brothers to record with me which I still listen to at home.

While I recognize that these days, everyone considers themselves an artist of some type, for me, this was a step towards my own greatness. When thinking about my calling, passion, and gifts, I realized I had been a writer for years before I even thought of writing a book. Those late nights, early mornings writing lyrics prepared me and gave me the discipline to sit down and write "My thoughts" in a more helpful and meaningful way. How awesome is that?

With this book, I hope too that you're able to take the examples provided, the support and encouragement and use it to motivate and create a skill that will lead you to greatness in the home, community and anywhere else you may want to succeed. As I got older and started to focus on school, music had to take a back seat. I started internships and volunteering in Indiana combining therapy and music. It occurred to me that I cared more about helping others than I did about recording my own music. So, while I used the encouragement and support I got from others seeing potential in me, I began to fall in love with seeing potential in others. This is so important because you will know that you are growing when taking care of yourself is no longer enough and you want to make others around you great as well. I took my passion for making music and started to give others an opportunity to experience what I experienced. This to me is what success looks like. When you're helping others grow and start to make sacrifices for the good of others. This is not saying that you don't make sure that you're successful; it's just saying that success doesn't just come from financial gains but also from giving and sharing with others.

Like my father did by sharing his free time with other

kids in the neighborhood or my parents taking in foster kids. Without others sharing with us, we wouldn't have much success. My brothers donating their computers, studio equipment, money and support helped me to learn to do the same for others. While in College, I met a guy named Mike who always put the success of others before himself. Mike is a charismatic and fun-loving guy. His goal in life was to make others happy and I gravitated towards him and we instantly became friends. My friendship with Mike taught me so much about chasing dreams because he believed in my potential so much. I do not think I have ever met a person like Mike and I am blessed because of our relationship. He's what some people would call a right-hand man. Mike's role in my life and the life of many other people he has come in contact with is to build confidence which as I told you earlier in the book is an area of weakness for me. This is a gift and talent that many people do not possess but Mike has this gift. With Mike in the room, he makes you feel like you could do anything. He makes you comfortable in your own skin. To this day, I leverage this relationship because I want to bring that feeling to anyone that I counsel or coach. I want to make people feel like they can do anything in the world. People are placed into your life to make you a better version of yourself while also growing your faith. Leverage the Mikes in your life today for success tomorrow, learn from what they are saying, see what they see in you, and capitalize on it.

Chapter 11

When Kevin Durant took his talents to Golden State, I was just as shocked as most of my friends. We spent hours discussing this decision and how it impacted the NBA and his greatness. All across the internet, people were giving their opinion about Kevin's decision to leave OKC and join an already stacked Golden State Warriors team. Whether you agree with Kevin's decision to leave OKC or not, he did leave and he has his reasons. When you're thinking from the perspective of success and achieving your goal, Kevin's decision doesn't seem that farfetched. If you're looking at your goals, your decisions should be based on the best opportunity to achieve your goal. We all define insanity as doing the same thing over and over again expecting different results. Think about your own life. In school when a group project was required who did you want to work with? When you played a team game and you had to pick teams, who were you trying to pick? The idea is put yourself with the people that give you the best chance to achieve success. Because of Kevin Durant's decision, he returned to the NBA finals, achieved his goal and was named MVP of the finals. No matter how anyone feels about it, Kevin Durant is a champion, his talent is unquestionable and he will continue to achieve greatness.

Now, place yourself in the shoes of Kevin Durant for a second. If you had a chance to join up with some amazing, talented and supportive people, who would you pick? Name at least five people who you believe are capable of providing you with support towards your success. Name some father and mother figures, friends and family members that you believe possess qualities that will help you to be successful at home, in the community, and in business. Think about who those people are and be intentional about recognizing the strengths you like that you would like to adopt as you work towards your own success. List each name and start documenting each quality you like about them. For example, when I started writing this book, I listed my father as one of those major supports in my life and I jotted down some qualities I liked that I wanted to adopt. My father's giving spirit is a characteristic that I had already adopted from him which assisted me immensely in the social work field. It allowed me to connect with people because of my willingness to support people in need. It's also a characteristic he adopted from his father who was also a giving person. My uncle was a wise and humble man who learned how to communicate with others and tap into their emotions which led to his success with his business. When looking to achieve success, always surround yourself with the people who give you the best chance to win. I connected with my brothers who were also like-minded individuals looking to achieve success and supporting each other to improve as fathers, leaders, and businessmen.

All of these relationships provide leverage to win and will increase chances of success when tapping into the positive characteristics.

Section 3

Faith

Chapter 12

Although we have spent the last few sections discussing others believing, supporting, and encouraging you. I have to be honest that a huge piece is also about you believing in yourself. I struggled with self-belief throughout my thirty plus years, and even found myself leaning solely on others' beliefs in me until they stopped saying and showing they believed in me. I was falling off fast and badly. Even when it came to making changes for myself I didn't think I could get my act together. But I did believe in God and that was key. I believed He had a calling on my life and provided me with talents and gifts to share with the world. I believed that if I put my trust in Him that things would change for the better. Slowly they did begin to change. My marriage, my confidence, my constant weight issues all began to improve. As a kid, God and religion played a major role in my family. My parents made it a goal to have worship together every single morning. Whether we liked it or not, God was going to be a huge part of our lives and I am grateful for that strong spiritual upbringing. I am grateful because I believe God, though misunderstood by me as a kid, served as a fallback or safety net for me. Growing up, if I was in trouble or scared about something, I was taught to pray and everything would work out. There were times when it felt like praying, my worries worked and other times it felt like it didn't work but overall, I felt better knowing that I had God to run to when I was afraid or hurt. As I got older and started to build my own personal relationship, I started to experience God in a different way. I started to feel his presence in my life and I started to see success in multiple areas as our relationship grew. Some of the stories I would read in the Bible started to make sense in my own life and I started to see my own experiences explained through the scriptures. I often asked myself, how do other people deal with life if they don't have God to talk too? By the time I was twenty-three years old, my spiritual life and relationship with God had never been closer. It wouldn't stay that way for long but in that moment, I had felt a deep connection to a higher power no one could shake and still cannot be shaken by any man. That unshakeable connection was what I needed to finally tap into my gifts and answer my calling. This unshakeable connection is what ultimately saved my broken marriage, improved my health, and created this book you are reading. As we come to a new section of the book, I think it's important to break down the connection between success and spirituality and its importance. I believe there are many people who are rich financially, but poor mentally, physically, and spiritually. If your mind is dominated by poor areas of your life, then no amount of money will ever create true success. I believe that God designed a unique life experience for you that can only be achieved when you follow your calling and choose faith over fear. Your calling or purpose in life will in some way impact the people around you and provide others with leverage to win. So, when we choose not to follow our calling, we in turn become a barrier to others achieving their success. Leveraging to win works both ways in that, while others provide you with leverage, you also are providing leverage to others. There is no need for you to be the weak link in the chain of support. Your sacrifice of service may be the miracle someone else is in need of today.

Chapter 13

When I think about my calling, my mind always goes to my gifts. My gifts are natural abilities I have. It's a trait I was born with and came naturally to me. We were given these gifts to bring glory to God and to live a fulfilled life. Our gifts are our VIP access to our creator. It's a sure way to keep us connected to God. Through our gifts, we are in constant communion with God because we know that it is through Him that we have achieved. Gifts can and must be developed and nurtured or like so many examples in the Bible, will be lost. Our gifts are what we should use when walking in our calling.

When I was in college, I met a guy name Andrew, a musician who would later go on be an amazing minister of the gospel. This dude was outstanding. It was clear that he had a gift for music as a singer, drummer, organist, bass player and much more. Any instrument he picked up he could master in a matter of minutes, maybe hours. How do I know? I watched him do it! I remember one day just watching this already amazing piano player pick up the bass guitar one evening after church and in two hours start playing the bass as if he had been playing for years. I watched in amazement not able to even speak.

His ability to learn and understand music came naturally to him and he took the time to develop this gift and more. As he worked to identify his calling, he used his gifts to help others and spread the gospel. He recorded music, trained other musicians and even started his own church. Now as an ordained minister, he is a leading a congregation and continuing to use his gifts to plant churches and lead others to God.

I have another friend that I met in college who is a powerful speaker and a great father. He had a gift of positivity as I have never heard a negative word come from his lips. He was in school studying to be a nurse, but would take speaking engagements primarily on weekends or when his schedule allowed. One day, he invited me to hear him speak, and from the start of his message, I knew that this was his calling. Not only did this guy have a great message, but he had a powerful voice, I mean, this brother could sing. His confidence was high, he was able to engage the entire room and when he ended his talk, he had a line of people waiting to meet and talk with him.

When I finally had a chance to talk with him, I asked him how he could get up in front of so many people and deliver so effortlessly and he told me it was a gift. I told him I wanted to be a speaker one day and he told me that he saw it in me. We spoke for a few more minutes about his gift and then he shared with me some really good insight. He told me there were two reasons why he sings before he starts to speak. He told me singing gets everyone's attention and allows people to focus in on the message and that singing also helps to calm his nerves before he speaks. He continued to travel the country in his spare time using his gift to speak and connect with people but not as often as he would like to. Over the years, I would harass him about his gift and his calling until one day he called me and told me he was going to follow his calling full-time. These are great examples of following your calling and using your gifts.

Chapter 14

Identifying your calling can take some time to figure out or it can be very easy depending on how you develop your gifts. If the natural supports in your life also help to foster these gifts, it will make it much easier for you to find your calling. Therefore, it is important to recognize your gifts and tap into them. Tapping into your gifts will allow you to have a close connection to God and it will lead you to your calling, passion, and success. Are you a good listener? Do people find it easy to talk to you? Do you pick up things easily? Do you make people laugh?

Take some time and think about what your gifts are. Then consider tapping into this gift by using it as often as you can. Throughout my life, I have enjoyed writing. As a kid, it started with poems, then I started writing letters to friends and girlfriends, writing lyrics for songs, and even plays and stories. Now I am writing my own books. I am tapping into my natural gifts to help others which is my calling. I have other gifts as well that have helped me; for example, I am a good listener and communicator. These gifts help me in my calling every day and soon will help you as well.

One of the first steps I took in identifying my gifts was to sit and write down all the things I felt I was good at that came naturally. I also reached out to some family and friends and asked them to tell me what they thought I was good at. I received great feedback from family and friends and I jotted every response along with my own thoughts onto the paper. I then thought and wrote down everything I was passionate about. I also wrote down what I wanted to do that would leave an impact in the world. I created this list and used my responses to identify my calling and work with a purpose to achieve my goal. God put a specific calling in my life and allowed me room to create how I would to follow in my calling.

I have been able to write books, speak to large groups of people, and provide deep coaching and counseling for individuals, families, and children. I have been blessed with the opportunity to be a husband and father, a child protective service investigator, crisis interventionist, mentor, and leader in my home, community, and church. I thank the creator for all the great opportunities and experiences I have been afforded. I also recognize that when I was not connected to the creator, my relationships suffered, and as a result my gifts and talents plummeted and I was no longer having an effective impact. The moment I reconnected with the creator, everything about my life realigned. My relationship with my wife began to repair, my career took on a new meaning, my health became a priority and my friends and family began to encourage and support me again.

I often hear people say that they don't know what their calling is and I want to push back on that a little because I believe your calling requires you to step outside of our comfort zone. The challenging part for some people is that stepping out of their comfort zone feels scary. They want to experience their calling in a safe and protected space. Since stepping into their calling requires faith past what they can control fear holds them back. Unfortunately, your comfort zone doesn't grow you and it doesn't require you to have faith or a need for God. For example, one of my close friends is a social worker and talented singer. She loves to sing and can usually be seen singing with a praise team, a singing group or backup for an artist. Although my friend is happy and feels called to be a social worker, just imagine with me for a moment if she felt called and followed the call to become a full-time professional singer. I often wonder what her life would be like if she was given or created an opportunity to make a living by singing. Would she, do it? Is her love for signing so strong that she could do this even if she wasn't being paid? The answer might be yes. The challenge for my friend and may others like her in identifying and pursing their calling is fear. Fear of failing or fear of success. She would also have to believe in herself that she could do it and have the faith that God gave her the talent to not only bring glory to His name and joy to others but also be able to provide for her family. It would also require her to step out of her comfort zone and pursue her dream. The only way for her to truly know would be for her to step out on faith, which is outside of her comfort zone and pursue the calling using her gift. It would also require her to create and execute a plan. Just because you feel called does not mean you don't have to plan. I felt called to become a speaker and author, but being called isn't enough, I still needed to prepare and plan for it. I felt called to be a husband, but that wasn't enough, I still needed to plan and prepare. Your calling is right in front of you, but you still need to plan and prepare. The route issue isn't always in finding your calling but in preparing to walk in it. You already know what you are born to do; now it's time to execute. Step out on faith and watch your life improve the moment you do. Your confidence will grow, and you will help keep the chain of support going for others to leverage your gifts in order to win. Remember, your confidence shows when others believe in you. Your confidence grows when you believe   in   yourself.

Chapter 15

One of the most important things I think of when discussing gifts and why it's so important is the parable of the talents. If you have not read the parable of the talents you can find it in Matthew Chapter 25. The entire chapter is a good read. This story hits me hard every day and I use it for motivation daily. The deep impact for me comes from what happens when you allow your gifts to lay dormant. If you don't use your gifts, you will lose your gifts. If you abuse your gifts, you will misuse your gifts. If you don't develop your gifts, you won't develop your relationships. When I didn't use my gifts, my spiritual connection was gone, my ability to communicate effectively disappeared, and my confidence diminished. I had to tap into my gifts to reconnect with God and watched as my weight went down, my marriage improved and I received a raise at work. I am not saying that this is the only way, I am saying that this way works for me and may work for you. God never left me, I cut off my connection to him. Now that I am reconnected, using my gifts and working in my calling, I am living a purpose driven life. I am helping others every day and communicating, counseling, and coaching. I am building a healthy marriage with my wife and becoming an amazing father. My confidence has skyrocketed and the stutter I had developed in the last two years has completely gone away.

God gave us these gifts for us to use for His glory. It's

also to keep us connected to Him. I use my gift of listening to read and develop my parenting skills. I listen to my wife to understand her wants and desires, and I listen to my staff and private clients to create a safe and healthy work environment and experience. Most importantly, I listen to the word of God, whether it is at church, in my daily worship or through other books. I know what God has called me to do and He has given me the gifts to excel in it. God has called you too and He has given you the gifts you need to excel as a father, husband, brother, partner, mentor, father or mother figure or friend. Your calling will not fail. As men, some of the biggest barriers we face when it comes to achieving success is fear, vulnerability, and confidence. Fear of success and a fear of failure are both barriers. The fear of success and failure comes with a level of responsibility that scares many men and limits growth. Being vulnerable and stepping out of our comfort zone is also a barrier as many of us would rather wait for the perfect opportunity instead of creating the perfect opportunity. These areas of fear can be quelled by faith and confidence. When you're walking in your calling, passion and purpose, you will not fail. The reason the other servants who were given talents succeeded was because they put their talents into action. Their perception of the master was different. They believed the master had faith in their abilities. and trusted them with this task because the master knew they would be successful. The last servant didn't have confidence in himself or didn't believe that the master had confidence in him. Even though he was given a talent, he chose not to do anything with it but hide it. The master has given you talents and gifts. He has also given you a purpose to lead in your communities, churches, and home. Just like the first two servants in this story, if you apply yourself and work on the gifts, and talents that the master has given you, then you will succeed.

When I started to really ponder where my life was going, I found myself thinking about the parable of the talents. I started to feel a small voice telling me that I was the servant in the story who was given a talent but decided to bury it rather than invest it. I thought about the many talents that God had given me and how I had indeed stopped using them. The calls I used to get to speak had stopped. People had stopped coming to me for advice and no longer looked for my leadership. I had developed a stutter which would appear anytime I had to speak publicly and my confidence in myself and my abilities had declined. I knew that God gave me these talents in order to help others and to double my talents into greater things; however, I had buried them. I remember thinking that one day the master would return and ask me what I did with the talents He gave me. What had I done with all that I was blessed to have. The answer to that question was painful to say out loud. It was painful because I knew that I buried the very things that were meant to bring me joy and success. I buried my talents and along with it went my confidence, respect, sacrifice, work ethic and motivation. If I was to ever achieve success, not only would I have to pick back up my talents, but also all the mentioned parts of myself that I buried. It occurred to me that many of our positives attributes that we have been blessed with are often times wrapped up in our natural talents. The moment I started to use my talents, I saw my confidence grow. My faith that the master trusted me with my talents gave me leverage to win.

Chapter 16

In this chapter, I want to talk about faith in terms of relationships, perseverance, and confidence. Hebrews 11. My faith in God and His promises are a major factor in building my confidence and faith in myself to achieve my purpose and calling. Faith is such a pivotal piece of success because achieving success is not easy. Being a father, provider, husband, and servant of God, all require faith and self-confidence. It is a lot of responsibility that without God could feel overwhelming. At times even with God, it can feel overwhelming. The only thing that will get you through is faith in God and faith in His promises to fulfill your desires. The saying is that God never gives you more than you can bear. I believe this to be true and have the faith that it is true even when things do feel like it is more than I can bear. There have been many times where I just couldn't see my way out of a situation but I held strong to my faith and the situation always seemed to work out. When I was ready to leave my marriage, it was my faith in God that gave me the strength to give it another try. When I was fed up with work and being overlooked for promotions, it was my faith that things would get better that kept me going. Motivation will get you going but faith will sustain you.

I have faith that all things will work for good, for those who love the Lord. I have faith that walking in my calling and using my gifts will help to improve my marriage, my career, my parenting and my spiritual life. I have faith that my coaching and speaking career will take off and I will be able to successfully reach millions of people with my message. I have faith. I may not see it all right now, but I know it will happen. My weight has always been an issue for me, but I have faith that I will be a slim and trim guy. I believe it because God will grant me the desires of my heart and my experiences with Him have always worked out when I kept the faith and stayed connected to Him. There are certain distractions that should not happen when connected to God unless He allows it to happen.

For example, if I am connected to God that means that I am using my gifts to spread the message He has given me and leading my family. To spread the message, I have to spend time with God, read and research topics, spend time with my family, coach and provide counseling, write my books, eat balanced meals and exercise. Because this is also a passion of mine, I love doing it and don't feel bored, frustrated or overwhelmed. In order for me to spread the message and help others achieve the success, I end up managing my time more effectively because I want to make sure that I do my best for God. If I have a book to read, that cuts into my TV time. If I am not sitting on the couch watching TV then that means I am not eating and lying down. If I am not eating and lying down, it means that I now have the energy to work out. Having the energy to work out allows me to exercise and spend time with the family as we do this together. Building time together with the family in return helps me to be better connected to my wife and child. Do you see how this is all connected?

Your faith connected with your faith in action will

catapult you to success and limit those behaviors that distract and destroy. I also don't believe that faith is some magic pill that you take and everything is alright. But what I do believe is that faith allows us to trust that God knows best. It also teaches you to believe in yourself. To trust the promise and to believe that you can achieve. The Bible is filled with stories of faith in action and we have these stories to encourage us to pursue our dreams.

The best parts about faith to me are the confirmations. When I decided to give my all in my marriage, it took faith to believe that things would change even when things around me appeared to get worse. I started having morning devotion and I really wanted my wife to join me in this practice to show her commitment to our marriage. I told myself that if my wife was as committed to the marriage as I was then she would join me in the mornings. When I told my wife that I was going to be getting up in the mornings for devotion and asked her if she would join me, she told me no. I could not believe that she wasn't willing to sacrifice like I was for our marriage. I tried to argue that she needed to make changes if the marriage was to work. But she still refused and walked away leaving me standing there in shock. Although I wanted to give up right then and there, I decided to have faith and get up the next morning for devotion. The very next morning, I got up and the morning after and the morning after that. I got up and had devotion. While I began to read and pray, I started to see a change in me. I started to understand the love that God has for us and how it goes past my desire to comply with His request. I wanted to learn to love my wife the same way that God loved me. It became less about what my wife was willing to do and more about what I was willing to do for my wife. And in case you are wondering, a few weeks later my wife started to join me in the mornings for devotion. This was confirmation to me that God was in the midst of our marriage and He was going to make sure that we were alright. Having faith isn't easy for a lot of people. We think we have faith, but in fact we struggle to let go of the control we think we have in order to allow God to reveal Himself. I wanted to control the situation by making my wife join me for worship but, the moment I let it go and had faith, she joined me. If she would have joined me immediately, I would have missed a valuable lesson about God's love and I would have ignored the lesson He was teaching me.

Faith is preparing for what you can not see. It's having the title for the book you haven't written. Faith is buying the welcome mat for the house you haven't purchased yet. It's believing that what you need will be made available to you and preparing to receive it. Never forget, that faith without works is dead. Faith with action equals success.

Section 4

The power of love

The Greatest of All These Is Love

W hen you think about success and what it means to you as a leader wherever you are in life, it is important to talk about love and its potential to aid in your process. I have heard it said that love has no place in business, and I disagree with the statement. I believe it is love that drives us and strengthens us to push forward. Whether it be the love of money, or the love of notoriety, or maybe your love for yourself or someone else. Love is a key factor in success. For this section, I want to focus more on how the love others have for you, as well as the love you have for others, is vital to your success. It one thing to love someone or something and another thing to express that love with actions. Love requires action and we learn to measure how much we are loved by another person's actions.

There are already lessons learned and knowledge gained because of someone's love for you. The mere fact that we are alive today can be directly linked to someone's love. You see, someone decided to bring us into this world. Someone decided to sacrifice their body, social life, relationships, career and much more in order to give us a chance at life. Although not all actions demonstrate love, there is nothing like the love of a parental figure, friend or significant other. This section of this book will explore the impact of the relationship with mothers and significant others in our lives. The goal of this section is to be able to identify the supportive model in our lives that elevate us as men to the next level. The areas of growth we need to develop from both mother and father are important, however, it appears most men are/or were being raised by women. This impact on us men has also been discussed in the previous section and may have had bearing on picking our significant other or choosing to remain single. Our social engagement and ability to connect with others can also be an added benefit or detriment to our success. Our ability to communicate with others or people of authority could affect our ability to advance in our careers, marriages, and leadership. This section will also look at my experiences with my mother, significant others and how these relationships have aided in my career, marriage, and leadership abilities.

This section will also demonstrate our importance as men in the world. The dynamics of our intimate relationships as a boyfriend, father and husband are usually directly linked in some ways to our family dynamics. Our music, movies and books paint pictures glorifying single parent homes, making as much money as possible and disrespecting women. We have been praised for chasing money instead of raising our children and being faithful husbands. We have watched our mothers struggle and in return have done the same to mothers of our children. The idea of putting others first has fallen far out of our minds and no one is interested in sacrifice and hard work. We all want glory, success and fame but not if it means that we must be held responsible, accountable and dependable. We run from the responsibility of fatherhood, we ignore the accountability as husbands and play the comfort zone of dependability. If we instead accepted our responsibility, we would accomplish everything that we want. It starts with learning to love and sacrifice.

Chapter 17

If I could redefine the word "mom," it would be defined sacrifice. Mothers sacrifice a lot. My mother is an amazing woman who endured a lot from her childhood into adulthood. She was born into a family with twelve other brothers and sisters in a small town in Trinidad and Tobago. She migrated to New York City where she married my father and had my two sisters and myself. I am her only son, and with my father working as much as he was, my mother assumed a lot of the responsibility for taking care of us. She enjoyed teaching us and making us into better versions of herself and my father. My mother is a warrior, always has been, and though we didn't always see eye to eye, she was also my biggest supporter. She knew early on that she wanted better for my sisters, and she and I wouldn't let anything get in the way. As a boy growing into a young man, I gave my mother her fair share of heartache and pain, however, my mother never gave up on me. It was my mother who forced me to play football in high school when I didn't want to. She forced me to go to college when I had plans of working at a local restaurant and becoming a manager. I had my father's work ethic and learned to be persistent and push past adversity from my mother.

My mother instilled some practices in me that to this day have enhanced my success. It was my mother who forced me to balance my checkbook. My mother who made me save sixty percent of my paychecks since I started working at the age of fourteen to pay household bills and budget for the things I wanted. While I wasn't perfect in keeping all the lessons she taught, when I needed to focus on getting things done, I have been able to draw from these lessons to provide for my own family. She is also very creative and this has proven key for me in learning to make something out of nothing.

Growing up in New York City, we did not have a lot of money, so in order to have a great time and not feel like we missed out on all things in life, my mother would come up with some creative projects to entertain us. It is that creativity that I continue to draw from when managing supervisors and developing recent graduate level social workers. Anyone I supervise, I try to make their professional development plan as unique and creative as possible. I want them to dream as I was able to dream and develop. My mother's creativity knew no bounds. Whether it was in the kitchen, or at the park or library, my mother worked tirelessly to get us to think for ourselves and be creative.

She wanted to see my siblings and I succeed. Her love for us pushed her to sacrifice and toil over our well-being. Through this type of love, I completed my bachelors and masters and went on to do some really great work in the social work field. The things I accomplished at my age in a female dominated field is an achievement that I owe to the love and support of my mother. Many of you have stories of things your mother sacrificed for you already. It's easy to ignore that and focus on the things your mother lacked or times you didn't feel loved but, dwelling on those things won't always aid in your success. It's about finding the areas where her love and sacrifice aid in achieving success. The physical lessons she showed to you by going to every game or helping with the science project. The times she forwent sleep or gave up her needs for yours. This kind of love will aid in teaching you some of the same patterns and behaviors. It's learning to recognize and understand that the sacrifices made for you will assist you in learning the sacrifices needed to grow yourself. Anyone who takes the time to pour into your life is someone you need to recognize and leverage the lessons learned to win. When I wanted to take the leap into working for myself, I leveraged the lessons my mother taught me to budget and limit my spending. When I grew tired of writing, I leveraged the words of one of my teachers who told me how good my writing was and that I should keep at it. These relationships are important and need to be leveraged always for success. My mother is a God-fearing woman who has her foundation rooted deeply in her faith. The lessons I learned from her and the characteristics I emulated have truly helped in my marriage, career and spiritual life.

She is the life of the party wherever she goes. She speaks well and can hold a conversation with anyone. Throughout my life, I would hear kids and adults talk about how awesome my mother was, and I looked at them wondering if we were talking about the same person. She knew how to make people feel welcomed and comfortable. I definitely leverage this every day when coaching and counseling.

My mother being a homemaker during my childhood also helped me to become a father to my daughter. Her daily sacrifice taught me the importance of addressing my child's needs over my own. Her round-the-clock care and self-discipline helped me to form important habits of hard work and follow through. My mother is an excellent example of self-sacrifice. There are not many mother and son relationships that I have encountered in my life that are not close. I rarely hear of a son that is not talking to their mother or has anything ill to say about their mom. That conversation is usually left for the father. Yet, when it comes to relationships with other women in our lives the level of respect and their value seem to diminish. As men, we tend to hold our mothers in high esteem and treat other women with less respect. It's the same age-old conflict that many men face in marriage.

When I first got married my wife and I had a huge fight. I had just come home from work and my wife wanted to go to the bank with me to add her name to my accounts. I was hesitant to do this because we already shared an account together and I didn't see the point of it. She told me that if something happened to me that she would need access to the account to pay bills and access money. Even though this makes perfect sense to me now, at the time I looked at my wife like she was crazy. I told her that nothing would happen to me and that if something did happen to me then my mommy would take care of her. Looking back at this memory now I realize how much of an idiot I was. My wife lost it. She looked at me as if I had lost my mind. I just stared back. I told my wife that my parents were my beneficiaries and that my plan was to have them take care of any needs she had. Because this is meant to be a wholesome book, I will leave out some of the pleasantries my wife hurled my way but just so we are clear, I took my wife to the bank and also made her my beneficiary. The real crime was not realizing that when you take a bride, she becomes the most important woman in your life. As men, it is important to hold all women in high regard and with respect. The love and respect we have for our mother should match for all other women in our lives. If you want to succeed in relationships then take this nugget of advice and watch your relationships improve. Having the right woman in your corner could mean the difference between success and failure.

Chapter 18

When I was a kid, basketball was my life. It was my everything. I carried a basketball with me, spent as much time at the park as allowed, and practiced in my free time. My love for basketball could be seen on the clothes I wore, the way I walked, and even in how I saw the world. My weekends were scheduled around church league and community league basketball games. In church, I had on the three-piece suit with gym clothes underneath. I ate, slept, and breathed basketball. I can admit that I was not a great basketball player. I wasn't terrible, but I never saw professional basketball in my future. The game just brought me a lot of joy.

When I finished grad school, I wanted to lose some weight and I wanted to have fun doing it. So, my friends and I got together and started our own summer league. Each of us tapped into our different skills and the outcome was full uniforms, recorded scoring stats, player of the day and week, excel spreadsheet, website and videos. Team meetings were called, players were seen before and after games practicing, and what started with ten players grew into a forty-player summer league. Amazing things can happen when people share a love of something. Love inspires change and creates opportunities. Passion and drive are built with love.

Although I don't play basketball anymore, my passion and drive have shifted. I apply the creative skills I acquired along the way to fuel my new love, goals, and missions. When it's a passion, it doesn't feel forced. It feels fun and exciting and I want to invest my time, money and life into it. My goals are to tap into the love a mother has for her child and apply that drive to my own passions. Love creates sacrifice and sacrifice bares success. How do I know? It's simple, I am alive! My mother sacrificed to have me. I cannot name a time in my own life where there was a success without sacrifice. Can you name a time in your life where there has been a success, small or big without sacrifice? There have been times when someone has sacrificed for you without you even knowing but there has been a sacrifice. Many of the books I read on the success point to love and sacrifice as two important aspects to success.

For over ten years, I worked hard to support someone else's dreams and goals. I was able to do this because part of my own dream and goals were linked with theirs. I went to school to be a social worker. I wanted to help others which was all I cared about when looking for work. While each job I held had aspects of my goals and dreams it never quite fit. I enjoyed my work and even shared in some success and promotions, but my ceiling was capped and so was my potential. When I looked for a job and found something I felt completely fit my passion and goals, I ended up competing with up to three hundred other people for the job; three hundred people who were also looking for a job that closely matched their purpose and goal.

During that time, I had multiple coworkers telling me I should venture out on my own but fear and insecurity plus comfort kept me at my job. I think it's important to recognize that if you're working for someone else that you also recognize that you are supporting someone else who dared to follow their dreams. I am not saying that there is anything wrong with supporting someone else's dreams, we addressed this in the other sections including this one but you are reading this book because you're looking for something. So, let's just put it out on the table. Are you in your current job because of comfort? Security? Fear or just to get out of poverty? Do you feel like you are living your purpose? Are you in love with what you do? Would you do what you're doing even if you weren't paid? Think about it. This is why love is so important because you go hard for what you love. You will practice, study, and push yourself for something you love. And we already said love equals success. I love writing and I love sharing my life and stories with others so writing this book was not hard. For me, it was fun and I enjoyed sharing the stories along the way. I also love to see others succeed. I knew once I got to a place in my life where others were succeeding and I wasn't happy for them that something was wrong. There is so much joy in my heart when I see my friends and family succeed. I love it so much I got into the coaching field to help other people dream, believe, act and achieve. I started by calling friends and family and asking them if I could coach them for free. One of my friends told me that I had been coaching since college and wondered what took me so long to do it professionally. The true answer is that I was afraid. I was afraid to venture out on my own. I was afraid that people would think I wasn't smart or good enough. I was afraid to succeed. I was afraid to fail. But love, love conquers all. My love for my wife got me out of bed in the morning for personal time and worship. Love for my daughter pushed me to put the unhealthy drinks down and start drinking water. Love for myself motivated me to pursue my dreams. And my love for God gave me the confidence to envision success. Love for my friends and family motivated me to write this book, Love truly conquers all. When things are done in love, people begin to see your good intentions. When love is at the center of what you do, people can notice. Sometimes it comes out as passion and excitement and other times it comes across as honest and genuine. When a man is in love everyone can tell and it cannot be hidden. When you love your job, wife or girlfriend, no one will question it because your actions will show it. So, make love a focal point in everything that you do and watch your success grow. Don't waste your time and effort on something that you don't love. Find a way to love it and watch how much easier everything will become. I didn't always enjoy reading books, but I understood the importance of reading and learned to fall in love with reading. I trained myself to read daily and now I love it and read something every day.

Chapter 19

As a man, I want better for myself and my family. I didn't always think that way though. Prior to college, I had no idea what my future held, and being a black man I didn't think I was going to make it to my twenty-first birthday. At the age of seventeen, all I cared about was making it to the next day. I didn't see a future and I didn't think about my future. Like most of my friends at my age, I was just going through life with no direction. My parents prepared me for life so I had the tools for success but I wasn't applying it. I was content with working at my part-time job, driving my dad's Chevy Astro van and hanging out with my friends. I didn't know any friends that were going to college or doing anything with their lives. My mother saw that I wasn't doing much of anything with my life and so she did two things. My mother asked my sister to complete a college application for me to the University she was attending and my mother also took both Kevyn and I to sign up for the national guard. She was very clear about one thing. We were going to do something with our lives.

My mother was disappointed in many of my choices at that time because she had given me all the tools I needed to succeed yet I didn't appear to be applying them effectively. I mean none of my friends had a checking account, credit cards or cell phones. But I had a cell phone, credit card, savings, and checking account. Because she pushed me to save money,

I had over five thousand dollars in my savings account by the time I graduated high school. These small yet effective tools and lessons proved to be valuable in achieving success. It's the idea of taking the tools provided and attaching them to what you love. Prior to college, many of my decisions were based on my parent's opinions, but once I entered college I was left to make my own decisions.

The other important lesson I learned from both parents is allowing success to be celebrated in the home, community, and church. My parents always pressed the importance of this. It's easy to see success in your current or future career, but success at its highest level allows you to lead and impact all three areas. These are all areas that were once dominated by men, and now we are lucky to have any men in the home, church, and community.

Doing what you love may not always be enough. Applying your gifts, talents and drive to what you love is the key. While in college, I was able to tap into my talents, use my gifts and be creative to a point.

As you read earlier in the book, I had no intention of going to college. My mother was hearing none of that and made sure I not only went to college, but that I finished and obtained a degree. While in college, it was my first time really being on my own and it felt great. While other people were busy going to parties, drinking, and getting caught up in drama, I was busy trying to find out who I was and enjoying my independence. I guess because I had already indulged in some reckless behaviors before college, I didn't see the need to go wild in college. I spent the first two years in school focused on recreating myself. What I found out was that I had a strong love for music. I loved writing my own raps and listening to music. I started recording with some friends in my sophomore year and I couldn't stop. It became a passion and though I wasn't the greatest it became all I wanted to do. As a kid, I always wrote poetry mainly because rap was not allowed in the house. My parents wanted no part of hip-hop in their house. While I did enjoy reggae, soca, and calypso, it just wasn't something I could rap too. College gave me the opportunity to explore more about myself and try things out.

I took full advantage of this opportunity and recorded as often as I could. So, if you are one of those kids that can't wait to leave home. Make sure you take advantage of your college experience. As far as I am concerned, if all you gain while in college is your degree then you missed out on some great networking opportunities. The majority of my professional career opportunities were created by some connection to college. I either got a job through someone I went to college with or have a shared friendship with a person from college that leveraged an opportunity. Leverage your college relationships to create opportunities for personal and business connections in order to win. One of my brothers from college started speaking as a leadership expert, and when he created his own conference, he asked me to join him as a coach. Another college friend of mine started her own business and cleared office space for me to use for free to see personal clients for coaching and counseling. These college connections have been instrumental in my success. College was the lifeline for many other people to connect with like-minded people who had a dream for success and teamed together to make that dream a reality. I leveraged my college connections to create my own business and chase my dream.

Chapter 20

Being a successful husband and father was a challenge for me from the start. I knew if I wanted to be good counselor, coach, and speaker especially to men, I would have to work on my marriage. I started to read as many books as I could on being a better husband and leader in the home. I made a promise to myself and my wife that I would train every day to be a better husband. I started to implement many of the recommendations I read and noticed some significant changes. I started to see my wife as a queen and treat her as one. The more I saw her value and appreciated her, the more I wanted to love her. As things improved in our marriage, we started evaluating our marriage on a weekly basis. We scaled our communication, intimacy, and parenting on a scale of 1 – 10. And discussed what was working in the marriage and what wasn't. Every week, we took time out to discuss these areas of the marriage and it really helped to improve the marriage. We live in a day and age where the rates of divorce are high and people are moving in and out of relationships like they are speed dating. Marriage is hard work and you should not take the decision to get married lightly. I would also recommend you don't take the decision to date someone lightly either. Take your time and write out all the qualities that make you a good boyfriend or husband.

Before any changes happened in my marriage though I had to evaluate myself and my own actions. This isn't always easy for men to do because we think we are simple humans and easy-going people. I had to seriously challenge myself to love unconditionally and put the needs of my wife before my own. I started waking up in the morning before my wife and joined a morning devotional call. The call consisted of nearly fifty people from all over the United States looking to revise their life. I took this call seriously and started making important changes. I stopped complaining about everything and started to be more understanding and patient. I focused on working on myself and becoming the best version of me. Today, my wife and I share a happy and loving marriage where we communicate effectively, make time for each other and grow individually and collectively as a couple. I learned it is important to be your best self and give your best at all times. When you focus on being your best you, you will not be so worried about others being their best. It wasn't until I worked on myself that I was able to be happy in my marriage. We tend to think that the woman is the problem, however, no one is a problem we are just different. If you are not happy, instead of looking for someone else to change, start by training to be the change yourself. I was unhappy in my marriage because I wasn't taking care of my health, I did not value myself and I had strayed far away from my calling. The moment I got back on track with my calling, my eating habit changed, I had more energy and I was genuinely a happy person. As a happy person, I didn't complain as much, I wanted to go out and do more and my wife wanted to be around me again. It really starts with finding yourself and connecting with your calling.

So, let's review.

Fall in love and love your work. Think of the love and

sacrifices made for you and apply the same principals to your own work. Take the drive you had as a kid for your hobbies and apply that drive to your adult dreams. Find what you love and create a plan to effectively achieve it. Eliminate the negative thoughts and increase the positive thoughts. I cannot stress how important a positive mental attitude is when pursuing your dreams. So often in my counseling and coaching sessions, I listen to my clients talk with so much negativity that I wonder if they knew that negativity only creates more negativity. Having a positive outlook on life with a positive mindset will take you much further than being negative ever will. Hearing the comments like "nothing ever works out for me" or "I am just unlucky" only creates more opportunities to feel unlucky and never have anything work out. However, there is more success when a person makes positive comments about themselves. Have you heard of any successful people who gave credit to a negative mindset for achieving a goal? When I am conducting a coaching session, I always emphasize the power of having a positive mindset. If you want to succeed in your marriage or career then start thinking those positive thoughts and envision success. Plan for the success by actively planning and pursuing it with a positive mindset. Negativity never helped anyone succeed.

Conclusion

As we close this book, I want to emphasize how important Fathers, Friends, Faith and Family are to our success. As men, we are the foundation of the world. We must accept a certain level of responsibility for what happens here on this earth and therefore we must be prepared to rise up and lead. As you tap into your gifts and begin to explore your purpose and calling, you must be intentional in being a fixed figure in the home, church, and community. We must also take the time to connect with each other and build on hopes and dreams. We tend to connect on a level of sports, music, cars, and women, but it's usually at surface level. We avoid going deep with each other and that has to change. We need to talk about our marriages, our career goals, fatherhood, and education. We need to uplift each other and encourage each other to pursue our goals.

There is so much strength between all of us that if we would work together we could change our world for the better. Part of my mission as a success coach is to provide men with the tools to dream big and achieve their goals. To help men tap into their gifts and create plans for implementation that will allow for success in multiple areas of their lives. While this book will be a benefit to anyone who reads and applies the principals, it was written for men. It was written to shift the current state of events and put the focus back where it belongs. It was written to bring a society that has seen the largest disappearance of men being active in church, communities, and homes this world has ever seen. That's my passion and I can't tell you why I am passionate about this. Perhaps I could look back at my own life and point out some things. What I do know is God has called me to speak on it and do something about it. It's true that many of us are not using, misusing and losing our gifts due to inactivity. Now is the time to activate those gifts and become the men that God has called us to be. Whether you are young or old, rich or poor, right now is the time for a change. If you are already on this path then this book was just reassurance that you are doing what you are supposed to do. If you're not on the path then use this book to identify your current natural resources and begin the journey of finding success and being at your best. If you are interested in rebuilding yourself and joining the "Leverage To Win" men's group, then email me at Dalton@newhopeclinical.com or visit my website www.daltontbeckles.com and subscribe to my mailing list.

At the beginning of 2017, I was handed a book by a friend with the title, Re:Vision. He let me know that there would be an early morning phone call with the author that I could join for twenty-one days. I was excited to get the book because I had heard the author speak before and it was one of his messages that ignited a fire within me to make some changes in my life. The book was a daily devotional and I was able to read it in its entirety before the early morning calls began. Prior to this book, I was getting up for work with barely enough time to shower and make it to the office on time. However, in order to make the calls, I had to go to sleep a little earlier and wake up earlier each day. Participating in these phone calls was actually pretty good, and because I was already up before everyone else in the house, I started to pray in the morning and even make breakfast.

At the end of the twenty-one days, the morning calls stopped but I kept waking up at the same time and decided to just make that my new time for self-care. I would get up, shower, have worship, cook breakfast for the family, read and make it to work with time to spare.

When I finally decided to follow the calling that I believed God had on my life, I instantly had the confidence to pursue it alone, and once I was able to pursue it on my own, all the support I needed came to my side. I realized that if I had continued to leverage my relationships inappropriately rather than believing in myself and my ability that I probably never would have achieved success in any of the areas of importance in my life. Ultimately, no one can want you to succeed more than you want to succeed for yourself. My marriage could only heal if I wanted it to heal. My career could only take off if I was in the driver seat. Once I took hold of my life then all the key relationships took their place as copilots. Cordelle, using his gifts and talents helped me build an office space in my home. My brother, Pierre, connected me to my first official speaking engagement. My father and mother gave me some startup money to furnish the office space. My good friend Lesly-Anne opened her office space up to me so I could conduct coaching and counseling sessions without charging me a dime. And the list goes on. There have been many other people who have stepped up to support me the moment I decided to take my life into my own hands. The moment I started to leverage my key relationships effectively, I started to win.

Without those key relationships and a firm belief in

myself, this book probably would not have been written. My marriage may have ended with my weight ballooning and my health declining. When I started to leverage my personal relationships effectively, I was able to use the relationships to learn, grow, develop and have accountability for myself. The relationships should support your growth not determine it. If you are waiting for the right person to be your leader rather than you as the leader yourself, it will be a challenge to fully achieve success. Friends and family can point you to success but they cannot achieve success for you. Besides, what do you do when the person you are holding on to can no longer carry you? What becomes of your life and goal? We all have a calling and purpose in life and the purpose and calling are unique to you. If you are to be successful then you must be confident in your calling and allow God to be the only person ahead of you.

The End.

To the Reader:

When I started writing this book, my intent was to target American Males ages 17 – 35. I chose this population because my own personal journey to becoming a man was formed and fashioned during those ages. These were the years in which most of my life experience would be pulled from. For me, it represented the start, middle and end of one journey and the beginning of a new journey using the same gifts and passions. That age range saw the best and the worst of me. When I started this new journey, and decided to write this book, I had been reading as many self-help, motivational, and success books as I could afford. The books I read were helpful and confirmed my calling and purpose. After a while, two important thoughts started to stick out in my mind.

The first thought was that many authors were all writing the same things calling it by a different name and becoming best sellers. The second thought was that I didn't feel like anyone was writing specifically for me or people like me. The ordinary individual. The person who was doing well enough in life, making decent money or working a job they loved but wanted something more. The person who came home every day and spent time with the family playing monopoly. The person who stayed mainly to themselves, but every once in a while, would show up to a church event. That person, I called us the safe zone people. You know who we are. It seemed to feel like we wanted to stay unnoticed. The problem with this is that staying unnoticed or safe usually is outside of your purpose and calling. Your calling is usually something that you are passionate about but also grows you as an individual. Your calling will present the meaning of your life and why you are here. To get the benefit of this book, you must first recognize that there is a calling and purpose for your life. To find out what your calling and purpose is, simply think about the parts of life that you are passionate about. Also, think of the gifts and talents that seem to come easy to you and infuse the two. For example. An author takes a topic that they are passionate about and uses their talents to write a book on that topic. A cosmetologist who enjoys making people look and feel better combines their talent of doing hair and make-up to create happy people. A doctor takes his passion for fixing people and combines that with their gifted hands to become a surgeon. The list goes on, but there will come a time where if you are not living your purpose or following your calling that you will start to feel uncomfortable, jealous and unfulfilled. Let's start the journey of embracing the important relationships around us to achieve success and walk in our calling with a purpose.

What I hope you achieved from reading the book.

My hope is that you can apply these steps to your own life and begin the journey of dreaming, believing, acting and achieving. Whether it's in your home, your community, your church or all three places. No matter your age or circumstance there is always time to make a change that will benefit you in these areas of your life. Your willingness and ability to achieve success in these areas will prove beneficial to your health, your family life, your confidence as well as your own financial well-being. I have a passion in my heart and soul for men. We live in a country where the impact of men in the household, community, and church are at an all-time low. Many of our children are growing up without a father or father figure. As a man myself, it's important that I play a part in painting a different picture than what is currently identified. Many of you reading this book grew up in a home without one or both parents present. The statistics are astounding in showing the effects of fathers not being in the home. The statistics are so alarming that I felt it my responsibility to talk about it. I talk about it because we do have a responsibility to our children, to our churches, our families and ourselves. I do believe that without fathers, husbands and leaders, we will only continue to see the decline of our nation. My hope is that we return to our rightful positions and lead the charge in creating a healthier world for our children, family, and friends. It is in your toughest moments that God will give you Leverage To Win.

Acknowledgements

First, I want to thank God for His grace and mercy, if not for the Lord, I don't know where I would be. Like Peter, I had taken my eyes off the Lord but He didn't let me drown. I thank Him for a second chance.

There are so many other people to acknowledge at this time. My beautiful wife, Melanney, my amazing daughter, Sarai, and my dog, Midnight. You all have supported me and helped to make my vision for success clear. I also want to acknowledge my family, friends, Pathways to Housing family, and my Omega family.

I would also like to acknowledge my accountability partners, Adavid Broden and Derrick Williams. My business partners, Adrian Gale, Alexis Harris, Ash Harris and Morganne Brownlee. My Millionaire Mindset Mastermind group members, Pierre Quinn, David Defoe and Michael Adu. Last but not least, Lesley-Anne Bovel and the entire TTC family who embraced me and supported me with the tools I needed to achieve success.

To all of my future business partners and supporters, I acknowledge and thank you in advance. I live by my words and I know I will be creating and building new partnerships and friendships that will give me leverage to win.

Book Recommendations

Think and Grow Rich (a black choice): By Dennis Kimbro, Napoleon Hill

The Success Principles: By Jack Canfield

Know yourself like your success depends on it: By Michael Stawicki

Pound the Stone: By Joshua Medcalf

Choose Yourself: By James Altucher

The greatest salesman in the world: Og Mandino

Chasing Failure: By Ryan Leak

Outliers: By Malcolm Gladwell

The Dream Chaser: By Tony Gaskins Jr

The School of Greatness: By Lewis Howes

The Compound Effect: By Darren Hardy

The Carpenter: By Jon Gordon

The 5 Second Rule: By Mel Robbins

For Married Men only: By Tony Evans

The Secret to Success: By Eric Thomas

Re: Vision: By Pierre Quinn

The Heart of Father: By Ken Canfield

Fatherless America: By David Blankenhorn

References

Biddle, J. A. (2012). 10 Surprising Statistics Showing the Importance of an Involved Father. Retrieved from https://www.avvo.com/legal-guides/ugc/10-surprising-statistics-showing-the-importance-of-an-involved-father

Blankenhorn, D. (1996). Fatherless America. New York: HarperCollins.

Canfield, K. (1996). The Heart of a Father. Chicago: Northfield Publishing.

Morris, M. (2014). Black Stats African Americans by the Numbers in the Twenty-First Century. The New Press.

National Fatherhood Initiative. (2016). The Father Absence Crisis in America [Graph]. Retrieved from https://www.fatherhood.org/father-absence-statistic

Worksheets
Identify Your Supports

Mother _____.
Father _____.
Mother Figure _____, _____, _____
Father Figure _____, _____, _____
Brothers _____, _____, _____
Significant
Others_____, _____, _____

Goals
Long-Term Goal/Goals (2-5 years)

_____

_____

Mid-Term Goal/Goals (9 months – 2 years)

_____

_____

_____

Short term Goal/Goals (3 months – 9 months)

_____

_____

_____

What are you passionate about?

What are your gifts?

What are your talents?

What are you willing to do daily to grow your passion?

Who are some people you currently know that can assist you along the way?

What does success look like to you?

Three promises

1. Promise to your self

2. Promise to your family

3. Promise to a significant person in your life

Dream Team

Your Starting Five

1. Who and why _____

   _____

2. Who and why _____

   _____

3. Who and why _____

   _____

4. Who and why _____

   _____

5. Who and why _____

   _____

Passions, Talents and Gifts

What are your passions?

_____

_____

_____

What are your talents and gifts?

_____

_____

_____

In what way do you want to leave an impact on the world?

_____

_____

_____

Who do you need to connect with to achieve your goals?

_____

_____

_____

Three specific dreams I have. My dream is to..........

   1. I will have

      _____

      _____

   2. I will own

      _____

      _____

   3. I will create

      _____

      _____

   4. I will be

      _____

      _____

   5. I will become

      _____

      _____

   6. My Key Team can help me

      _____

      _____

For coaching, counseling or speaking engagements, email me Dalton@newhopeclinical.com or visit www.DaltonTBeckles.com

Leverage To Win

Key Relationships All Men Need To Succeed

Dalton T Beckles

94401501R10065

Made in the USA
Columbia, SC
01 May 2018